MACROBIOTIC NUTRITION
A Guide to Sustainable Plant-based Eating

EDWARD ESKO

IMI Press
LENOX, MA

The first wealth is health.
Ralph Waldo Emerson

Be careful about reading health books. You may die
of a misprint.
Mark Twain

All vegetal foods are virgin materials for the
purpose of maintaining and constructing our body.
Neither meat nor animal products are virgin
material for us. We must eat vegetables and their
direct products. This is the biological principle
and fundamental law.

George Ohsawa

MACROBIOTIC NUTRITION

Contents

MACROBIOTIC NUTRITION
A Guide to Sustainable Plant-based Eating
Text Copyright © 2019 by Edward Esko

ISBN-13: 978-1721970070
ISBN-10: 172197007X

Published by IMI Press
P.O. Box 2051, Lenox, MA 01240
InternationalMacrobioticInstitute.com

Third edition: November 2019

We can travel to any place on the planet in a matter of hours and communicate instantly with those on the opposite side of the globe. We therefore need the flexible, universal principles of macrobiotics to enlighten and guide us in the planetary era in which we live.

1 CYCLES OF NUTRITIONAL ENERGY

Nutrition is defined as the sum of the processes by which an organism obtains, takes in, and utilizes food. These processes begin with the change of inorganic elements into the organic material of plants. The organic matter of plants— carbohydrates, proteins, and fats—is then converted into both energy and physical substance when we eat.

Solar energy is stored in green plants and converted by us into cellular energy. This is known as the carbon cycle since it involves the extraction of carbon from the atmosphere and its release back into the atmosphere.

This cycle is a clear example of yang, or taking in, and yin, or release. Not only is the carbon cycle governed by yin and yang, it takes place in five stages. These five stages correspond to the cycle known in macrobiotics as the five transformations. The five transformations is a fundamental principle in the healing systems of ancient China and throughout the ancient world.

The principle describes the movement of the atmosphere in response to stronger or weaker sunlight. It is estimated that each square yard of the earth receives a thousand watts of solar energy each minute in the form of light and heat. Most of this free energy is reflected back into space or absorbed and reradiated a heat. Sunlight is highly energetic and dispersed, and corresponds to the state of energy known as "Fire." Fire is the most expanded or diffused stage of energy in the cycle. In the next stage—photosynthesis—plants absorb sunlight.

Energy from the sun combines with water and carbon dioxide from the atmosphere. Carbohydrates are the result of this more yang process. Chemically, photosynthesis is depicted in the formula $6CO_2 + 6H_2O + sunlight -> C_6H_{12}O_6 + 6O_2$. Translated, the formula reads: carbon dioxide plus water plus sunlight produces carbohydrate plus free oxygen.

In this process, energy becomes yang or condensed. Oxygen, which is strongly yin or expansive, is expelled, making the molecule of carbohydrate more yang. Sunlight, which is yang or energetic, is absorbed by yin oxygen atoms in the water molecule (H_2O). Oxygen becomes yang and thus less attracted to the single hydrogen atom, also yang, in the molecule. The molecule separates and the oxygen is released.

The remaining hydrogen combines with carbon dioxide to form carbohydrate in the form of glucose. Glucose is the first food made by green plants. Other nutrients, such as proteins and fats, are chemical derivatives of this basic compound. Living things depend upon the derivatives of glucose, both for energy and physical substance. The sunlight stored in glucose is the source of the biological energy that supports life. The process whereby sunlight is stored as glucose is endothermic, meaning that the glucose contains more energy than the elements that create it. In the five transformations, photosynthesis is a yang process of condensation and storage and corresponds to the stage of "Soil" or "Earth."

In the next process, known as biosynthesis, sunlight reaches its most yang or condensed stage. Here simple glucose is used to create more complex structures known as complex carbohydrates. These long-chain molecules form through the combination and bonding of many smaller glucose molecules. They exist in the higher plants in the form of starch. In cereal grains, for example, starch takes the form of polysaccharide glucose (in contrast to mono- or disaccharide sugars.) Proteins, minerals, and fats arrange themselves around this basic substance. In the five transformations, biosynthesis corresponds to the most yang or condensed stage in the cycle, a stage referred to as "Metal."

A reverse process begins when food is eaten and digestion begins. The compounds assembled during biosynthesis are broken down into their more basic components. Polysaccharides, which are complex sugars, are reduced to their original form, or molecules of simple glucose. Breakdown begins as food enters the mouth and continues as it moves through the digestive tract.

Enzymes secreted by the salivary glands, stomach, pancreas, and small intestine are responsible for the breakdown process. In the case of polysaccharide glucose, such as that of cereal grains, digestion takes place largely in the mouth through interaction with ptyalin, an enzyme contained in saliva. Proper chewing is therefore essential in extracting the energy and nutrients contained in foods. Polysaccharides are further broken down in the stomach, and then completely digested in the duodenum and small intestine. In the five transformations, digestion corresponds to the stage known as "Water." It is the first process in the breakdown and release of the energy stored in plants. It takes place in a liquid medium. Human beings are unique among other species. We have inserted another process in between biosynthesis and digestion.

That process is known as cooking. Cooking is a form of pre-digestion in which the energy of food is partially broken down and energized through the application of fire and water.

Cooked food is more energized than raw food and is easier to digest. Fermentation is another human invention. In fermentation, foods are broken down or "digested" by bacteria outside the body. Once foods are broken down into their most basic forms—for example, carbohydrates into glucose, proteins into amino acids, and fats into fatty acids and glycerol—they pass through the villi of the small intestine and are absorbed into the bloodstream. However, some foods bypass this process.

Refined sugar, or sucrose, made up of a molecule of fructose and a molecule of glucose, is a simple sugar. It enters the bloodstream almost immediately, causing imbalance and extreme compensatory reactions. With absorption, the process known as metabolism begins. Metabolism involves complementary yin and yang phases. The more yang phase, anabolism, consists of the building up of the body's substance. The more yin phase, catabolism, involves the breakdown of nutrients so as to extract their energy. Catabolism occurs at the cell level through a process known as respiration, in which the sunlight stored in plants is released as free energy.

Oxygen is the fuel for the conversion process and is provided through breathing. Carbon dioxide and water, the elements required by photosynthesis, are given off as waste products.

11

Respiration corresponds to the stage known as "Tree" in the five transformations. Sunlight is released from glucose and waste products are produced. The energy released in this process is used by each of the body's cells and ultimately returned to the environment. From the point of view of the movement of energy, photosynthesis and biosynthesis are the yang "capturing" phases of the cycle. Plants conduct these processes. Digestion and respiration are the yin, "releasing" phases, and represent the stages of water and tree respectively. Animals perform these processes. The carbon cycle is but one of many examples of the beautiful complementarity existing between plants and animals.

To sum up, the carbohydrates in plants provide us with stored energy from the sun. This energy exists in a highly concentrated form in the complex carbohydrates found in cereal grains. The point of eating is to break down these complex molecules and release the energy they contain. That energy is used to animate all of our life functions, and especially our consciousness and thinking centered in the brain. Consciousness exists as light particles produced by the brain. These particles originate with sunlight captured by whole grains and other plant foods.

Whole grains and other plant foods are ideal not only for our physical health and radiance, but also for the maintenance and development of human consciousness in its fullest dimensions.

A human body in no way resembles those that were born for ravenousness; it hath no hawk's bill, no sharp talon, no roughness of teeth, no such strength of stomach or heat of digestion, as can be sufficient to convert or alter such heavy and fleshy fare.

Plutarch

2 THE SECRET OF BALANCED NUTRITION

Among plants, cereal grains have an ideal balance of nutrient factors. Optimal balance takes the form of a one to seven ratio (one part yang or contraction to seven parts yin or expansion.) That ratio counterbalances the amount of energy coming in to the earth from the sun, planets, stars, and cosmos (seven), with that being radiated outward from the planet and back into space (one.) Cereal grains closely approximate the one to seven ratio. We see it in the proportion of minerals to proteins, and proteins to carbohydrates they contain. These nutrients, known as macronutrients, make up the bulk of our daily intake.

Other nutrients, such as vitamins, minerals, enzymes, and bacteria are known as micronutrients. Their intake is much less than that of the macronutrients. Fats are counted among the macronutrients. Fats are counted as either protein or carbohydrate, depending on their source and use in the body.

Let us look at common foods so as to see which ones are of themselves more balanced, and which are extreme and unbalanced.

ONE TO SEVEN COMPARISONS*			
Food	**Mineral (ash)**	**Protein (fat)**	**Carbohydrate**
Rice	1.2	7.5/1.9	77.4
Wheat	1.7	14.0/2.2	69.1
Millet	2.5	9.9	72.9
Soy	4.7	34.1/17.7	33.5
Beef	0.8	16.9/26.7	0
Azuki	3.0	21.5/1.6	58.4
Broccoli	1.1	3.6	5.9
Squash	1.4	1.4/0.3	12.4
Apple	0.3	0.2/0.6	14.5
Salmon	1.4	22.5/13.4	0
Shoyu	20.8	5.6/1.3	9.5
Miso	14.9	12.8/5.0	21.0
Tofu	0.7	7.8/4.3	2.3
Egg	1.0	12.9/11.5	0.9
Ham	0.8	15.2/29.1	0
Sugar	trace	0/0	99.5
Cheese	3.7	25.0/32.2	2.1
Human Versus Cow's Milk			
Human	0.2	1.4/3.1	7.1
Cow's	0.7	3.5/3.5	4.9

*Grams per 100-gram sample

In the above chart, One to Seven Comparisons, derived from USDA and Japan Nutrition Association food composition tables, we see that cereal grains (brown rice, whole wheat, and millet) most closely approach one to seven in their ratio of minerals to proteins to carbohydrates.

Keep in mind that the measurements in these tables are averages. No two grains of rice are exactly the same as are no two eggs or slices of beef. Squash, in this case winter squash, and other vegetables are not as near to this ratio, and neither are apples. Although fine as supplemental foods, we don't recommend eating them as principal foods.

When analyzed from the perspective of one to seven, these tables reveal much about our daily eating habits. Some foods are inherently balanced, while others are one-sided and out of balance. Some require little in the way of compensation. Others can only be balanced by the intake of opposite extremes. Let's take some examples.

Beef and eggs, for example, are mostly protein and fat and are lacking in minerals and carbohydrate (see chart above.) They are one-sided and unbalanced. When eating a hard-boiled egg, the peeled egg is often held in one hand, and the salt shaker in the other. Salt is sprinkled liberally on the egg before each bite. Without the salt, the egg is flat and tasteless, with salt it becomes more enjoyable.

By shaking salt on the egg, people are attempting to supply the missing minerals and bring the food more into alignment with a one to seven ratio. The same thing occurs when a person eats beef. Salt is added to hamburger patties, or high-sodium sauce is sprinkled on steak before or after cooking. Again, these measures are attempts to compensate for a lack of minerals. Without salt, such high protein foods are rather tasteless.

Japanese restaurant food offers another example. The most delcious cuts of raw fish, or sashimi, are usually those with the highest fat content. Fatty tuna and salmon are prized for their smooth soft mouthfeel. They practically melt in the mouth. These foods are high in protein and fat. They are lacking in minerals and contain no carbohydrate, again, a departure from the one to seven ratio. That imbalance helps explain how these foods are served and enjoyed.

When eaten as is, fatty tuna or salmon are not especially delicious. They become delicious when dipped in shoyu, or soy sauce. Shoyu, as we see in the table, is high in minerals, especially salt.

That is why it is used in moderation in macrobiotic cooking. Then, as we see in the table, salmon is lacking in carbohydrate. White rice, which is essentially pure starch, is often eaten with fatty fish to provide the missing carbohydrate. White rice more complementary to fish, while brown rice is better with vegetables, including plant proteins such as tofu or tempeh.

For many, however, the starch in white rice is not sufficient to make balance. Sashimi or sushi are thus often served with sake, or rice wine, which is high in sugar, or with beer, which also high in carbohydrate. In many cases, even that is not enough. At the end of the meal, fresh fruit, often citrus, is served, as is a dessert such as tiramisu or green tea ice cream. These help supply the missing carbohydrates and round out the meal. Following this, green tea adds the necessary liquid to make the balance more complete.

Going back to the example of eggs, a breakfast centered on eggs is unbalanced. It is heavily weighted toward fat and protein. Eggs don't have enough salt or minerals to balance the protein. Enter a food such as bacon. Bacon is cured in salt, and that is one reason some people find it delcious, as the salt makes up for the deficiency of minerals in the pork protein. At the same time, salt-cured bacon providess salt that is lacking in the eggs. That is one reason why bacon and eggs are a popular combination. Now, what about the missing carbohydrate? That is provided by orange juice, fried potatoes, ketchup, and coffee with plenty of sugar. Still these additions don't approach a one to seven equilibrium. More carbohydrate is needed, and that explains the popularity of the mid-morning coffee break. What about the family grill or barbecue? Salt is added to ground beef patties and processed hotdogs and other meats.

Together with the extreme method of cooking over an open fire, this contibutes to the carcinogenic, or cancer-causing properties of processed meats. Hamburger or hotdog buns supply some of the missing carbohyrate, but not enough. Additional carbohydrate comes from ketchup, mustard, sugared relish, lettuce, tomato, onion, pasta or potato salad; and for the adults, plenty of ice cold beer or wine. The kids make balance with ice cold soda and extra helpings of ice cream.

What is the result of such a chaotic approach to making balance? Plenty of excess in the form of too much fat, too much protein, too much simple sugar, and not enough balanced whole foods.

This extreme way of eating completely skips over more balanced whole grains, beans, and other plant foods. The negative health effects are becoming increasingly clear. The modern epidemic of obesity is only one among the many negative results of the modern diet.

A healthy way of eating is based around foods that are inherently balanced, or in other words, foods that maintain a balance that is close to one to seven. It is precisely those foods that make up the core of a plant-based macrobiotic diet. We see that on average, 100 grams of whole brown rice contains 1.2 grams of mineral, 9.4 grams of protein and fat, and 77.4 grams of carbohydrate.

These percentages are close to one to seven, meaning that whole brown rice is, in and of itself, a highly balanced food. How does whole wheat compare? Whole wheat kernels average 1.7 grams of mineral, 16.2 grams of protein and fat, and 69.1 grams of carbohydrate. Wheat has nearly twice as much protein as does rice.

That is one reason whole wheat products such as bread, noodles, pasta, seitan, and others are valuable additions to a plant-based diet. Soy products fill a similar need. Soybeans average 4.7 grams of mineral, 34.1 grams of protein and 17.7 grams of fat, and 33.5 grams of carbohydrate. Compare that to beef, which contains 0.8 grams of mineral, 16.9 grams of protein and 26.7 grams of fat, and 0 grams of carbohydrate.

Or compare soybeans to eggs, which are at 1.0 grams of mineral, 12.9 grams of protein and 11.5 grams of fat, and 0.9 grams of carbohydrate. Soybeans have roughly twice as much protein as beef and nearly three times the protein of eggs. That is one reason traditional soy foods such as miso, natto, shoyu, tofu, yuba, and others are valuable additions to a plant-based diet. When compared to grains, beans, including soy and azuki, are lower in carbohydrate. That is one reason why they go well with brown rice and other whole grains, which help provide the needed carbohydrate.

It also helps to explain why azuki beans are often cooked with sweet vegetables like squash or with natural sweeteners to create delicious and satisfying dishes and even desserts. That is also why a food such as miso, which combines soybeans with grains such as barley or rice, is a balanced whole food. So far we have been talking about the quantity of nutrients in common foods. Now let's take a look at their quality.

The fats in grains and beans are mostly unsaturated, meaning that they are liquid at room temperature. So when you store olive oil in your pantry or even in your refrigerator, it exists as a liquid that pours freely from the bottle. That is not true of the fats found in beef, eggs, cheese, and other animal foods. The fats in these foods are saturated, meaning they are solid at room temperature. Saturated fat is responsible for many problems in the body.

It accumulates in the arteries and blood vessels, contributing to atherosclerosis, or "hardening" of the arteries. This condition underlies the widespread epidemic of cardiovascular illness we see today, and can be traced back to the modern diet. In macrobiotics we say that saturated fat is yang or solid, while unsaturated fat is yin; diffused and liquid. Saturated fat comes mostly from yang animal sources, while unsaturated fat is found largely in yin plant foods. Molecules of saturated fat are filled with yang hydrogen atoms, while unsaturated fats contain fewer hydrogen atoms, leaving gaps in their structure.

The gaps in the atomic bonds in unsaturated fats makes their physical properties more soft and flexible. Saturated fats thus produce hardening and thickening in the body's cells and tissues, while, when eaten in proper proportions, unsaturated fats promote softness and flexibility.

Although not shown in the table, vegetables are excellent sources of minerals, vitamins, and fiber. Fermented vegetables, such as sauerkraut and pickles, are good sources of beneficial lactobaccillus and other helpful bacteria, sometimes referred to as probiotics.

Vitamins such as Vitamin C and E, which are abundant in green and yellow-orange vegetables, are not present in noticable quantities in grains and beans, and that is why these vegetables are excellent complements to a grain-based way of eating. Fresh, organic, seasonal fruits, when consumed as snacks or desserts, also help supply necessary vitamins.

There are many discoveries to be made by applying the one to seven analysis to daily foods. These will be revealed and discussed in future volumes. Before closing this chapter, however, I would like to point out differences between human milk and cow's milk and explain why human milk is ideal for human infants. Cow's milk has three times more minerals—0.7 versus 0.2 grams—than human milk. One mineral, calcium is needed by the infant calf for rapid bone growth following birth. For humans, that quantity is excessive.

Studies show that the calcium in human milk is more bioavailable than that in cow's milk, meaning that it is more readily absorbed and utilized in the body.

Excess calcium from cow's milk circulates in the bloodtream and is deposited throughout the body, leading to problems such as kidney stone, calcified breast tissue, and calcification of the pineal gland. Next, cow's milk is higher in protein than human milk, but that is not necessarily a good thing.

According to Viva.org.uk:

> The protein content in 100g of whole cow's milk (3.3g) is more than double that of human milk (1.3g); this is because the amount of protein in milk is linked to the amount of time it takes that particular species of animal to grow in size.
>
> Growing calves need more protein to enable them to grow quickly. Human infants on the other hand need less protein and more fat as their energies are expended primarily in the development of the brain, spinal cord and nerves. Species with the highest milk protein concentration exhibit the most rapid growth rate.
>
> Cow's milk contains 3.3 grams per liter and the calf doubles its birth weight after 40 days. Human milk contains 0.9 grams per liter and the human infant, the mammal with the slowest growth rate, doubles its birth weight after 180 days. The weight gain of calves during the first year (0.7-0.8 kg per day) is nearly 40 times higher than that of breastfed human infants (0.02 kg per day.)

In cow's milk, the ratio of the yang protein known as casein to yin whey protein is inappropriate for humans.

The ratio of casein to whey in human milk is 40 to 60; in cow's milk it is 80 to 20. Cow's milk contains far more casein than human milk. This yang protein is hard to digest. (Because of its yang, sticky quality, casein is used in the manufacture of glue.) The casein in cow's milk has been linked to a variety of diseases, including type 1 diabetes, allergies, and some cancers.

In terms of quantity, the fat content of human milk is roughly equivalent to that of cow's milk. However, there is a huge difference in the quality fats these milks contain. Studies show that 100 grams of cow's milk contains 2.5 grams of saturated fat, 1.0 grams monounsaturated and 0.1 gram of polyunsaturated fat. Human milk, on the other hand, contains 1.8 grams of saturated fat, 1.6 grams monounsaturated and 0.5 grams of polyunsaturated fat. Cow's milk has a higher level of saturated fat than human milk, while human milk has more unsaturated fat. Again, according to Viva.org.uk:

> The higher level of unsaturated fatty acids in human milk reflects the important role of these fats in brain development. In humans the brain develops rapidly during the first year of life, growing faster than the body and tripling in size by the age of one. The brain is largely composed of fat and early brain development and function in humans requires a sufficient supply of polyunsaturated essential fatty acids.
>
> The omega-6 fatty acid arachidonic acid (AA) and the omega-3 fatty acid docosahexaenoic acid (DHA) are both essential for brain development and functioning. Both are supplied in human milk but not in cow's milk.

25

As we see, both on the quantitative and qualitative levels, cow's milk is actually not suitable for human infants, or for children or adults for that matter. From the beginning, macrobiotics has recommended breasfeeding for infants and the adoption of a plant-based, dairy-free diet.

3 TO COOK OR NOT TO COOK?

Proper cooking is essential. Cooking adds energy to food and accelerates the release of energy and nutrients. Cooking is a form of pre-digestion that helps break down plant fibers so that we access stored energy and nutrients.

It is important to understand what cooking is. The nutrients in whole grains, beans, and many vegetables are not so accessible in their raw uncooked form. Grains and beans are especially hard and tough. Cooking softens them and makes the nutrients they contain more accessible. It is the first step in the breakdown of food into energy and nutrients. There is a great difference between human beings, who cook food, and animals that do not.

Have you seen the movie *Chimpanzee*? The chimps have their own culture and history. There are different tribes. The tribe featured in the film was in a good position. They lived in and controlled the nut grove.

The chimps' main food is fruit, but fruit is lacking in protein. Nuts, which contain protein and fat, were an important supplement to their diet.

Because chimps are intelligent, they developed the ability to use tools to obtain necessary protein. They learned how to crack the hard shells by striking them with a rock. To get even more protein, they invented another method. They took a twig and stuck it into an anthill. When they pulled it out, it was covered with ants, which they would then eat for their protein.

The chimps did not cook their food. They did not use fire. Their life is somewhat miserable and narrow compared to ours. When it rains, they must endure the cold and damp. They have no warmth and shelter. Plus their living space is small; their natural habitat is limited to a small section of the tropical forest, compared to the unlimited range of human settlement on the planet. There is a vast difference between humans and chimpanzees: grain eating versus no grain eating, the use of fire versus no fire.

4 RICE AND WHEAT

Whole cereal grains are the primary foods in a plant-based macrobiotic diet. Within the realm of whole grains, there are two main categories: one is brown rice and the other is whole wheat. They are the yin and yang of cereal grains. Rice is the primary grain of Asian cultures, while wheat is the staple food in the Middle East, Europe, and America. The difference between these two staple grains is vast; it determines the very nature of the cultures and civilizations that eat them.

Most of our friends are enjoying brown rice on a daily basis. Most are happy eating it daily with condiments and side dishes. It can be eaten as is and is sweet, chewy, and satisfying. You only need to boil or pressure cook it and serve it along with your other dishes. By eating whole unrefined rice as your main food, you are receiving all of its nutrients in their intact and balanced form. How about whole wheat? I can remember when I started macrobiotics many years ago. I experimented with whole grains.

When it came time to try whole wheat, I bought some whole-wheat berries and boiled them as you would brown rice. That was my grain for the day. Wheat. As I quickly discovered, wheat kernels are very chewy. They have a somewhat tangy, and not a particularly sweet taste. Wheat is higher in protein than rice, with about twice as much protein.

Many thousands of years ago, our ancestors got tired of chewing the tough wheat grains. Being very inventive, they developed brilliant techniques for crushing or milling grains into flour. Milling opened the door to a whole range of wonderful and enjoyable foods, such as sourdough bread and noodles, which in comparison to wheat kernels, are incomparably fun (i.e. noodles), delicious, and user-friendly.

However, what happens when you crush the grain into flour? Number one; life energy goes out. Number two; the flour begins to lose nutrients through oxidation. As a result, more side dishes, including animal food, are required. Western culture is characterized by wheat and animal food. With whole brown rice as your main grain, however, you can get by with fewer animal products. That is one reason why we recommend brown rice as a main grain with whole-wheat products reserved for secondary use. The rise in gluten sensitivity is largely due to the development of high-yield hybridized wheat and other grains. Hybridized wheat is known as "dwarf" wheat. Heirloom wheat, which humanity has eaten for at least 10,000 years, is a delicate yin grass.

Its gluten, or protein, is relatively easy for the digestive system to break down. When eaten in moderation, it normally poses no problem for digestion or absorption. The primary wheat products in a macrobiotic diet include unyeasted sourdough bread and organic noodles and pasta.

Baked flour products and boiled noodles have opposite effects on the body. Baked products start out as soft flour and after baking become hard. Noodles and pasta are dried and hard before cooking. After boiling, however, they become soft, especially when served in soup or broth.

Because of that, noodles and pasta tend to be easier to digest. Noodles tend to keep the body flexible, while baked flour products, especially those that are hard and crunchy, can cause tightness and rigidity when eaten in excess.

Compared to the yin, more expansive and delicate nature of heirloom wheat, modern hybridized dwarf varieties are yang. They are small and readily absorb yin fertilizer. Up until the last century, the human digestive tract has had no experience in processing them. Writing in *The News Herald*, Theresa Edmunds describes the problem with modern wheat:

> Wheat has been hybridized during the last 50 years to such an extent that it has increased the gluten content exponentially. Not only that, hybridization has created new strains of gluten—one study found 14 new ones. Why was wheat hybridized? Originally it was to increase production and create hardy, pest-resistant wheat with a long shelf life.

The man credited with breeding the high-yield dwarf wheat that is grown today is Norman Borlaug, who won the Nobel Peace Prize in 1970 for his work. Through this hybridization process, the gluten content increased but no testing was ever performed on animals or humans. The problem with gluten is that it is hard to digest and with wheat now containing so much of it, it is becoming a problem for many people.

There are several ways to reduce or avoid the problem of gluten sensitivity. First, avoid modern wheat products; second, base your diet on brown rice, millet, and other gluten-free whole grains and grain products; and third, shift to heirloom organic wheat, barely, and rye and the natural products made from these important staples as soon as your digestion becomes strong enough.

Each grain, including those containing gluten, has a unique beneficial effect on body and mind. Our goal is to be able to enjoy the benefits of all of them without restriction. By selecting our foods wisely and preparing them with insight and awareness, we can establish health while gaining dietary freedom. That freedom is the goal of a macrobiotic way of life.

5 BROWN RICE BASICS

When we cook brown rice and other whole grains, we are utilizing the basic elements that make human life possible. The first is the rice itself. For our temperate climate, we suggest using short grain organic brown rice as the primary grain. Other rice can be used for variety or to adapt to seasonal variation. The rice we use is mostly from Lundberg Farms in the Sacramento Valley of northern California. The Sacramento Valley has a unique environment that is well suited for growing rice.

The Sacramento Valley lies between two mountain ranges. To the east lies the majestic Sierra Nevada, while the Pacific Coastal Range lies to the west. Beyond the Coastal Range is the Pacific Ocean. During the winter, the snowpack builds up along the peaks of the Sierra Nevada.

In the spring, the snow and ice melt, sending highly charged pure mountain water cascading down toward the Valley. This water collects high above the Valley in an artificial lake know as Lake Oroville.

Lake Oroville is the product of the man made Oroville Dam, one of the largest earthen dams in the world. From Lake Oroville, pure mountain water streams down through irrigation channels to the floor of the Valley. That highly charged mountain water nourishes the rice fields. That is one reason why Lundberg rice is so exceptional.

Pure clean water is also essential when cooking brown rice. Water quality has become a huge headache in the modern world. Municipal water is chemically treated and often fluoridated and is not suitable for daily use. The lakes, rivers, ponds, and streams of North America were once perfect for drinking. Now they are highly polluted. As a result, we recommend using natural spring or well water.

Decades ago, we would visit a local spring in the countryside and fill large five-gallon glass bottles with pure clean water. That water was used for cooking brown rice and other foods at the student house where I was living. Later, during the years I lived in the Berkshire Hills of Massachusetts, we would visit a spring nearby and fill bottles with fresh clean water. Unfortunately, by that time, the glass bottles we used before were no longer available, so we were compelled to use plastic. Certainly not ideal, but the quality of the water was so superior that we accepted this compromise. In any case, try to secure the best quality water for cooking brown rice. Filtered water can be used if natural spring or well water is not available.

Salt is the next essential element. Try to locate high quality natural sea salt. Grey salt is not recommended as it has too high a content of magnesium. After experimenting with a variety of natural sea salts, we selected Si Salt, processed from the clean Pacific waters off Baja, California as ideal for daily use. Keep in mind that when adding salt to your brown rice, only a pinch is needed.

The fourth essential element is fire. As with water, the quality of fire is often problematic in the modern world.

Cooking with fire has been replaced with artificial electric ranges and microwave ovens, both of which impart unnatural and potentially harmful radiation and both of which take away the delicate control necessary for healthful cooking. For this reason we recommend cooking over a gas flame. (Note that most gourmet chefs reject electric cooking in favor of gas cooking.)

Our ancestors kept in contact with fire on a daily basis. Fire is essential not only in cooking but also for warmth and shelter. We are the only species that has tamed fire (both for creative and for destructive purposes.) Taming fire was the first step in gaining mastery over our natural environment. I feel sorry for those who are cut off from regular contact with fire because of electric stoves and microwave ovens. The long thread of human tradition stretching back into the untold past, based on the use of fire, has been severed.

I advise all students of macrobiotics to master the preparation of brown rice as a first step toward health and freedom. Please gain the ability to make perfect brown rice on a consistent basis. The rest of your cooking will come together in a grand symphony of natural harmony.

Basic Brown Rice (Tight-Lid Boiling Method)

1. Wash one cup of organic brown rice by covering with water, rinsing, and draining the water. Repeat three times.

2. Place in a pot with a tight-fitting lid. Add a small pinch of sea salt (optional) and 1 ½ - 2 cups of spring water.

3. Cover and bring to a boil on a medium high flame. When the rice comes to an active boil, reduce the flame to low and cook for 50-60 minutes.

4. Turn off the flame and let the rice sit for several minutes.

5. Remove from the pot with a wooden spoon and place in a serving bowl.

Brown rice may also be cooked in a pressure cooker from time to time. Bring 1 cup of washed grain to a boil in 1 ½ cups water and when pressure is up, place a flame deflector under the pot. Lower the flame and cook for 50 minutes. Brown rice and other whole grains can also be soaked prior to cooking, anywhere from one to several hours or even overnight depending upon one's condition and needs.

6 REFLECTIONS ON THE SANDWICH

In a recent class we studied the differences in physical condition and mentality that arise from eating whole grains such as brown rice, and those that arise from eating flour products, especially bread. The focal point of our study was the sandwich. The conclusions of our study are actually quite profound.

According to Wikipedia:

> A sandwich is a food item consisting of one or more types of food placed on or between slices of bread, or more generally any dish wherein two or more pieces of bread serve as a container or wrapper for some other food. The sandwich was originally a portable food item or finger food, which began its popularity primarily in the Western World, but is now found in various versions in countries worldwide.
>
> The sandwich is considered to be the namesake of John Montagu, the 4th Earl of Sandwich, because of the claim that he was the inventor of this food combination. The *Wall Street Journal* has described it as 'Britain's biggest contribution to gastronomy.' It is said that Montagu ordered his valet to bring him meat tucked between two slices of bread, and others began to order 'the same as Sandwich!'

Lord Sandwich was fond of this form of food because it allowed him to continue playing cards, particularly cribbage, while eating, without using a fork, and without getting his cards greasy from eating meat with his bare hands.

In macrobiotic thinking, cereal grains are the foundation of human life and health. They comprise what is known as *principal food*. However there is a profound difference between eating grains in their whole form and eating them in the form of flour, regardless of whether the flour is refined or whole.

Brown rice and other whole grains with the outer husk still attached have been known to sprout after thousands of years. However, when you crush a grain into flour, which is essentially a fine powder, life energy disappears and the flour begins to oxidize and lose nutrients. Because of these deficiencies, it can no longer serve as principal food.

With the invention of the sandwich, grains, primarily wheat, were relegated to *secondary foods*. The role of grain was downgraded to that of a mere carrier or vehicle for something else, quite often meat or other animal food. Our daily bread was no longer the staff of life but now became a convenient wrapper for beef, pork, chicken, eggs, and cheese. The focus of the sandwich is not the bread, but the inner contents. Moreover, with the creation of refined flour and white bread, the grain lost all value as a staple food.

Not only did the sandwich downgrade the role of cereal grains in the human diet, it also obscured the central role of eating itself. According to Wikipedia: "The sandwich's popularity in Spain and England increased dramatically during the 19th century, when the rise of an industrial society and working classes made fast, portable, and inexpensive meals essential."

As did Lord Sandwich himself, people turned to sandwiches as a way to eat while doing something else, whether drinking, playing cards, driving cars, working at their desk, etc. Eating became something you did "on the go." Gone was the reverence for the sacred act of communing with nature and the universe. Gone was the family meal and offering of thanks or saying of grace before eating. The invention of the sandwich heralded the rise of cheap, low-quality fast food. With the decline of whole grain as principal food, eating no longer served to unify the family and society. Eating became an increasingly individual and isolated act, with increasingly negative consequences for personal and planetary health.

The two most popular foods in America, the hamburger and pizza, are both hot sandwiches, with pizza being a form of open-faced sandwich. Both feature meat, cheese, and animal food as the main ingredient with the crust or bun relegated to a secondary role. Both are considered to be cheap, fast food.

Their popularity is directly linked to the current epidemic of obesity and declining health, as well as ongoing degradation of the environment. Don't get me wrong. I enjoy sandwiches as much as anyone. My favorites include crispy fried tempeh with yellow mustard and unpasteurized sauerkraut on organic sourdough bread; fried tofu with lettuce and cucumber on organic sourdough; and hummus with lettuce, onion, and black olive on whole grain ciabatta. However, in the macrobiotic view, sandwiches are an enjoyable supplemental food; not a replacement for brown rice and other whole grains.

Also, it is important to reestablish the central role of eating and reverence for food that, since the beginning, was the cornerstone of human civilization. Let us restore whole grains as the center of the human diet while pausing before eating to give thanks to nature and the universe.

7 SOUP AND STOCK

Why do soup and stock play such an important role in a plant-based macrobiotic diet? Why are they considered essential for health? There are a number of important reasons. The first is that soup prepares the digestion. That is why it is normally served at the beginning of the meal. Because it is primarily liquid, with ingredients that tend to be softer than usual, soup is easy to digest. As we all know, soup is often the first food served to someone who is ill.

These beneficial effects are augmented by the fact that soups are seasoned with naturally fermented products such as miso (organic soybean paste) and shoyu (organic soy sauce.) These foods contain natural probiotics that aid both in digestion and absorption, while increasing the stock of beneficial bacteria in the colon.

A second reason is that with soup, we can regulate our body temperature. This is especially important in cold weather. It is sometimes hard to guarantee that the various dishes in a meal will remain hot after serving.

However, we can usually guarantee that soup will be hot. Hot soup improves circulation and warms the body. It can restore vitality depleted by cold damp weather. Hot tea also serves this purpose, but without the nutrients in soup. Soup has a slightly salty taste. In macrobiotic cooking a salty taste is achieved by adding seasonings such as sea salt, shoyu, or miso.

These seasonings help the body, and especially the bloodstream, maintain a healthy alkaline condition. Simply put, soup builds strong blood. Healthy blood is the origin of a healthy body and of strong immunity, since immunity is carried by specialized white blood cells.

Moreover, many of the basic ingredients in macrobiotic recipes have specific blood cleansing and purifying effects; they help the body discharge excess fat, cholesterol, and toxins. These ingredients include dried shiitake mushroom, wakame, kombu, and other sea vegetables, and fresh chopped scallion used for garnish.

Healthy, nourishing, and delicious soups begin with a simple stock. The ingredients for stock include wakame sea-vegetable (kombu can be substituted on occasion) and dried shiitake mushroom. These ingredients are the foundation of soup and broth. To prepare basic stock, place dried shiitake mushroom (one cup per cup of water) and wakame (a one- or two-inch piece per cup) in cold water. Bring to a boil, cover, and simmer until the wakame and shiitake are soft, tender, and easy to chew.

As an alternate method, soak the shiitake and wakame separately for about 1-½ hours. Slice the wakame into bite-sized strips and do the same for the shiitake. You can remove the hard stem of the shiitake and the tough spine of the wakame for ease in chewing. Add the wakame and shiitake, plus the soaking water, to cold water. Cook as above.

An experienced chef knows by taste, aroma, and color when the vegetable stock is done and ready for seasoning. This ability can only be gained through experience. I recommend that you taste your stock after about 10 to 15 minutes of simmering. Don't forget, basic vegetable stock made with dried shiitake mushroom and wakame is the foundation for healthy and nourishing soup.

Unseasoned stock has a clean, pure taste with a subtle hint of the ingredients used in the broth. It should not be too strong, but fresh and light. It should have a light, delicate, almost clear color. If the stock needs more cooking, meaning that the vegetables have not yet become tender, let it cook longer but sample it every five minutes or so to prevent over cooking.

Once your stock has achieved perfection, it is time to add seasoning. You have one of two options. You can opt for a clear broth or a more full-bodied stock. The seasoning of choice for clear broth is high quality organic shoyu.

Shoyu is a rich dark liquid. It adds a wonderful slightly salty taste that blends perfectly with ingredients like wakame and shiitake. Since stock or broth is essential for health, use the highest quality natural and organic brands (contact the International Macrobiotic Institute for recommendations.)

Most high quality brands are handcrafted in small batches using techniques passed down from generation to generation. They use only the purest natural and organic ingredients.

The secret to good shoyu broth is to add a small amount at the beginning, less than you think you need. You can pour directly from the bottle into the broth. I call this "under-adding." Add less at the beginning and gradually add more if needed. After each pour, ladle or spoon some broth into a bowl for sampling. If it is fine, leave it as is. If it requires more, add more. Repeat until the broth is perfect. Remember, you can always add more seasoning, but if you over-add, you can't take away what you've added.

Properly seasoned clear broth has a light, translucent amber color and a slightly salty taste. You should be able to detect hints of the wakame and shitake. The saltiness of the shoyu should not overwhelm these subtle, delicate flavors. Adding miso creates a more full-bodied stock. Unlike shoyu, which is a liquid, miso is a thick paste.

The three main varieties of miso are mugi miso, made with fermented barley and soybeans, genmai miso, made with fermented brown rice and soybeans, and hatcho miso, made only with fermented soybeans. As with organic shoyu, we recommend using high quality natural and organic miso. Aside from these traditional varieties of miso, most of which are imported from Japan, you can also enjoy specialty miso.

Miso such as that made by South River Miso in Massachusetts and Miso Master in North Carolina are fine for regular use. For example our friends at South River invented several new types of miso such as dandelion-leek, chickpea, azuki bean, and garlic-red pepper miso.

The first key point in making miso soup is to properly dilute the miso paste before adding it to the broth. We do this by placing miso paste in a small bowl (usually one teaspoon per cup of liquid), spooning broth from the soup pot over the miso, and mixing until the paste is completely dissolved. Dissolving the miso allows it to spread smoothly and evenly throughout the broth without forming clumps. Our goal is to achieve a consistently smooth broth.

The second key point is the same as that for clear broth. "Under-add" at first. Taste a sample. If the taste is perfect, leave as is. If a stronger flavor is needed, add a little more, taste, and leave as is or add slightly more until perfect flavor is achieved.

Properly seasoned miso soup occupies that rare "sweet spot" in between bland and overly salty. Continual practice will help you identify and occupy that magical zone. Good miso soup is deep, rich, and satisfying. Try not to use too many ingredients in your soups and other dishes until you understand the energetic nature of each ingredient and the positive or negative effect of combing it with the other ingredients in the dish. In and of itself, there is nothing wrong with variety. I'm in favor of diversity.

Nature itself is nothing if not endlessly diverse and varied. However, in the quest for variety, be careful not to obscure the simple yet profound harmony that underlies all healthful cooking. "Keep it simple" is a good motto to keep in mind when cooking daily meals.

We need to master the basics before we get fancy. If we lack a clear, solid foundation, we risk becoming confused. Besides, macrobiotics is about living as simply and close to nature as possible and not becoming dependent on luxuries that can compromise our health. When learning to prepare soup and stock, I suggest that you first master the basic stock presented above, seasoning with shoyu for clear broth and miso for a more full-bodied soup. Once these basics have been mastered, we can enlarge the range of ingredients to include vegetables, whole grains, noodles, tofu, and others.

Although they share many characteristics, clear shoyu broth and full-bodied miso soup are somewhat opposite. Shoyu is clear; miso is thick and full-bodied. Clear shoyu stock lends itself perfectly as a broth for things such as cooked noodles or leftover brown rice. Fewer vegetables are added so as to make room for these hearty ingredients. Miso, on the other hand, lends itself less to hearty noodles and brown rice and more to a variety of vegetables. Hearty grains like barley and rice are in most

Noodles in broth are a macrobiotic staple. They can serve as a one-dish meal. They are fun, nourishing, and satisfying. In cold weather, they are warming and vitality restoring.

I can't imagine life without noodles in broth. Noodles in broth are an excellent way to use your basic clear shoyu stock. To prepare, boil organic noodles such as udon, soba, somen, or other varieties until they are ready to eat. Rinse under cold water.

Place in individual serving bowls and ladle hot broth over them to cover. Garnish with fresh chopped scallion or chive and enjoy. Once you master basic noodles in broth, you can add a variety of delicious, nourishing, and healthful toppings. Try adding things such as fried tofu, quick steamed greens, fried tempeh, battered and deep-fried vegetables and seafood (tempura), steamed or poached fish or seafood. Once again, you can use noodles in broth as a quick, one dish meal. After you add selected toppings, don't forget to garnish appropriately.

As we have seen, miso soup has a thicker, more full-bodied texture. Vegetables tend to complement miso broth, although grains and noodles can be added on occasion. Common vegetables and combinations include:

>Daikon, wakame, shiitatke
>Carrot, onion, wakame, shiitake
>Kabocha (sweet fall squash), wakame, shiitake

Of course there are many other combinations of vegetables, including leafy greens that contribute to nourishing and healthful miso soups. Root and round-shaped vegetables can be added to the cold water at the beginning, together with wakame and shiitake. Greens require less cooking and are best added at the end.

Once again we can't overemphasize the importance of strong nourishing stock and broth for overall health and wellbeing. Below is a summary of how to prepare basic miso soup and shoyu broth.

Miso Soup

1. Soak wakame (one-quarter to one-half inch piece per person) for about five minutes and cut into small pieces.

2. Soak dried shiitake mushroom (one mushroom per cup of liquid) for about five minutes and cut into small pieces, removing the hard stem.

3. Add the wakame and shiitake to fresh, cold water and bring to a boil. Meanwhile, cut some vegetables into small pieces. Add to the wakame and shiitake stock. Recommendations include: daikon; carrot and onion; sweet winter squash; and other fresh, local, and organic vegetables.

4. Add the vegetables to the boiling broth and boil for three to five minutes until the vegetables are soft and tender.

5. Dilute miso (one-half to one level teaspoon per cup of broth) in a little water, add to soup, and simmer for three to four minutes on a low flame.

6. Garnish each bowl or serving with fresh chopped scallion, chive, or parsley.

Simmer the soup for three to four minutes after you add miso to the broth. Don't bring the soup to a boil once the miso has been added.

The broth should not have a harsh salty taste. From time to time include leafy greens (kale, collards, watercress, turnip or daikon greens.) Add them toward the end of cooking. You may occasionally use leftover grain or noodles to make a thicker soup. Cubed tofu may be added to the broth on occasion, usually toward the end of cooking.

Shoyu Broth
As with miso, it is essential to use high quality organic shoyu (traditional soy sauce.)

Like miso, shoyu is an essential ingredient in strengthening digestion, maintaining healthy blood, and fortifying natural immunity. Those with gluten sensitivity may use organic gluten free tamari or other soy sauce.

1. Soak wakame (one-quarter to one-half inch piece per person) for about five minutes and cut into small pieces.
2. Soak dried shiitake mushroom (one mushroom per cup of liquid) for about five minutes and cut into small pieces, removing the hard stem.
3. Add the wakame and shiitake to fresh, cold water and bring to a boil.
4. Reduce the flame to medium-low and simmer until the wakame and shiitake are tender.
5. Add organic shoyu to taste. The broth should not have a harsh salty taste. It is better to start with a small amount and add more if necessary. Simmer for several minutes. Turn off the flame and serve.

Ladle the broth over cooked udon, soba, or somen for hot noodles in broth. Ladle over leftover brown rice for hot rice and vegetable soup. Add white meat fish for a nourishing fish and vegetable soup. Drink as is for a hot alkalizing broth. Vegetables such as daikon, onion, carrot, or leafy greens may be added to the basic wakame/shiitake stock. Shoyu broth should be garnished with fresh chopped scallion, chive, or parsley.

8 ESSENTIAL GARNISHES

If we were to go ahead and serve soup broth as is, without any further steps, quite frankly, our dish would not be "macrobiotic." Macrobiotics is about achieving harmony, balance, and counterpoint in our dishes. As we know, this is achieved through the application of yin and yang, or expansion and contraction. In the case of soup or broth, balance is achieved through garnish.

Let's analyze according to yin and yang. Miso and shoyu are both fermented foods. Fermentation is generally a yin process of decomposition and breakdown. However, miso and shoyu are salted and aged (yang) and these factors cause these foods to have an overall yang effect.

Dried wakame is a product of the salty ocean, and although it is one of the lighter sea vegetables, it is on the whole yang due to its mineral content and the drying process. Shiitake are generally more yin, as are mushrooms as a category. However sun drying makes them yang or concentrated. (Fresh shiitake are yin; softer and juicier.)

And, on the whole, the soup is cooked over fire, which is yang. The ingredients are first boiled and then simmered until tender. What quality of energy makes balance with this overall yang quality? The answer is yin; light, fresh, upward energy. Fresh chopped scallion provides that energetic balance. (Chive and other finely chopped greens can also be used.) Scallion has a relatively small root but large stem and leaves. Most of its growth takes place above ground in a yin or upward direction. It is green in color (green is more yin than orange, brown, or red), and is used raw, which is more yin than cooked. So, on the whole, the yin upward energy of raw scallion balances the yang concentrated energy of salty cooked soup; the green color balances the brown or amber color of the broth; and the fresh raw energy of the scallion balances the dried and cooked energy of the wakame and shiitake plus the aged miso. What is the overall effect of adding garnish? The effect is to catalyze, liberate, and activate the energy of the cooked broth, making it not only delicious and visually appealing, but also highly effective as a health supporting and healing food.

This is only one example. The applications of garnish are actually endless, since garnish represents the balance of yin and yang, the ever-changing order of the universe.

9 SODIUM VERSUS IODINE

On a recent trip to the seaside we stayed in a motel right on the beach. Sitting at night on the porch facing the ocean, I was struck by the two opposite energies emanating from the vast churning darkness. The first was the powerful smell of the salt water. The element sodium prevails in salt spray. Sodium is highly yang or constrictive. The other strong smell was that of iodine. In contrast to yang sodium, a concentrated metal, iodine is found in the plant world, specifically within sea vegetables. Iodine is the strongly yin complement to yang sodium. Like salt, the smell of iodine is powerful and unmistakable. Both are omnipresent at the shore.

Sea vegetables are a primary source of iodine, the element essential for proper thyroid function. Within a plant-based diet of whole grains, beans, fresh vegetables, and other whole natural foods, establishing a regular and appropriate intake of sea vegetables is of prime importance. The classification of common sea vegetables into yin and yang can help us understand how to make the necessary adjustments.

The classification of sea vegetables into yin (expansion) and yang (contraction) matches their classification according to their iodine content. Nori, the most yin of the sea vegetables, has the least iodine, while wakame, dulse, arame, hijiki, sea palm, and kombu have progressively more.

Kombu is highest in iodine and is the most yang of the sea vegetables. This follows from the principle that opposites attract. Iodine is a strongly yin element. It vaporizes into a purple color at relatively low temperatures. It balances the yang sodium in ocean salt. Sodium vaporizes into a brilliant yellow similar to the color of the sun. When you visit the ocean, the smell of salt combines with that of iodine to create a powerful yang and yin balance. As we can see, as sea plants become yang, from nori through to kombu, they attract and store increasing amounts of iodine.

Sea vegetable condiments, such as those from Maine, are a convenient way to help the body receive proper amounts of iodine and essential minerals. Iodine levels have decreased in recent years, dropping by as much as 50% due to depleted soils and the presence of elements such as bromine, fluorine, and chlorine that compete for iodine receptor sites in the body. The iodine in iodized salt is not fully bioavailable and sea salt contains almost no iodine, thus sea vegetables are becoming increasing necessary for health including thyroid health. It is well known that sea vegetables convey protection from radioactivity.

They contain substances that bind with radioactive particles (and other toxins) and cause them to be discharged from the body. Sea vegetables are especially beneficial in protecting the thyroid from the harmful effects of radioactive iodine. Larch Hanson, founder of Maine Seaweed Company, describes this process as follows:

> All went well until some nearsighted nuclear scientist started splitting uranium atoms and creating radioactive iodine-131 which concentrates through the food chain from grass to cows to milk to humans, and can end up in the thyroid, burning it out, leaving people unable to self-regulate their lives. Iodine-131 has a very short half-life of eight days. That means that within a period of two months, it emits most of its radiation. And if that iodine-131 happens to be situated in the thyroid while it is emitting its radiation, it will do great damage to the thyroid gland.
>
> The best long-term strategy is to integrate seaweed into one's daily diet. Then your thyroid will always have adequate levels of stable iodine-127 and will not take in radioactive iodine-131. Digitata kelp has the highest iodine content, followed by kelp. Alaria has moderate levels of iodine. All are good sources of iodine provided you don't roast them, releasing the iodine to the air. Nori and dulse don't contain much iodine, compared to kelp and alaria. Source: *Protect Your Thyroid* by Alex Jack, Planetary Health, 2011.

The power of sea vegetables to block absorption of radioactive iodine became apparent to me a number of years ago.

A young man with thyroid trouble came to see me for consultation. He had read about the beneficial effects of eating sea vegetables on the thyroid and began consuming them in amounts beyond those normally recommended. He went for a thyroid scan about a month later. He was given a pill that contained radioactive iodine, and then asked to wait as the iodine collected in the thyroid. The scan was scheduled for about six hours after he took the iodine pill. Several times during the waiting period, he felt the urge to urinate.

Then, when it came time for the scan, he was asked to lie on his back with his neck and chest under the scanner. The scan is used to detect the location and intensity of the rays given off by the radioactive material.

Normally, a computer displays images of the thyroid gland. In his case however, no image appeared on the screen. The doctors were puzzled. Apparently, his intake of sea vegetables had saturated his thyroid with enough stable iodine-127 to block further absorption. He had made himself immune to the effects of radioactive iodine and was able to discharge the radioactivity through the kidneys and bladder.

10 NO ROOM FOR JELL-O

Recently I had an experience in which I felt the taste and sensation of eating Jell-O, a long-forgotten food that I hadn't eaten in more than forty years. The feeling I experienced was that of Jell-O rising up from deep within and discharging. It happened out of nowhere and was unexpected to say the least.

Why, of all the dietary excesses of the past, would Jell-O take so long to discharge? Wasn't Jell-O that somewhat innocuous smooth, sweet, and refreshing dessert that people around the world ate every day? As the slogan went: "There's always room for Jell-O." Such an obviously yin food should, in theory, be discharged fairly quickly. But *forty years* to discharge?

In macrobiotics we classify foods into yin and yang; expansion and contraction, dense and diffuse, solid and liquid, etc. This classification is extremely relevant to health and happiness. To understand it better, recall the game "twenty questions" when we ask whether something is "animal, vegetable, or mineral?"

The mineral world, which includes salt, is highly dense and contracted. Comparing plants and animals, plants are part of the larger environment within which animals exist. Plants are therefore yin (expanded) while animals are yang (condensed). At room temperature, saturated animal fat is dense and solid, while unsaturated plant oils are light and fluid.

Jell-O is made from gelatin, or hydrolyzed collagen. Collagen is a main constituent of an animal's yang infrastructure. It is a group of naturally occurring proteins found in animals, especially in the flesh and connective tissues of vertebrates. Collagen is the main component of connective tissue, and is the most abundant protein in mammals, making up about 25% to 35% of the whole-body protein content. Collagen is mostly found in fibrous tissues such as tendon, ligament, and skin, and is also abundant in cornea, cartilage, bone, blood vessels, the gut, and intervertebral disc.

Now, where does the collagen come from that goes into gelatin and hence Jell-O? It is extracted from the skin, horns, hooves, bones, connective tissue, and organs of cattle, chickens, horses, and pigs. In other words, the waste products left over from meat processing that are not considered edible, at least not initially. (Google the image of *gelatin* for graphic examples.)

The foundation of Jell-O (gelatin) is extremely yang. Bones, hooves, and connective tissue are too yang to eat without converting them into a more yin semi-solid form. Thus they are hydrolyzed or chemically dissolved in water.

Collagen-derived gelatin comes from the yang core of the animal. That's why it takes so long to discharge. Yin foods tend to discharge quickly; while yang takes much longer. The body will discharge sugar and alcohol in a matter of days, while it takes weeks, months, and even years to fully discharge eggs, meat, chicken, and cheese.

Gelatin, made from the yang core of animals, has possibly the most yang point of origin among animal foods. Salt is the most yang or condensed substance among daily foods. Excess salt may take the longest to discharge. In extreme cases, it may not be possible to reverse the extremely yang effects of eating too much salt.

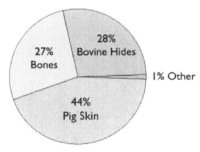

Materials Used in Gelatin Production

As Shizuko Yamamoto once told me, "it's easy to change fresh daikon into takuan (salt-cured daikon pickle), but impossible to change takuan back into fresh daikon." As do other animal foods, gelatin produces an overall hardening and rigidifying effect on the bones, blood vessels, and connective tissues.

Hardening in these regions interferes with the smooth flow of energy through the chakras (energy centers) and meridians (energy streams). This in turn results in diminished organ function and potentially in sickness, including stubbornness and mental rigidity. Animal excess accumulates throughout the body in the form of arterial plaques, as well as cysts, stones, and tumors. At the surface, it results in hard dry skin and growths such as moles and warts. For optimal health, it is essential to discharge accumulated animal food and restore a smooth and active flow of energy. Why is Jell-O so popular? Could it be that it has addictive properties? To answer these questions let's take a look at the standard list of ingredients in Jell-O:

JELLO, GELATIN DESSERT, LIME
INGREDIENTS: Sugar, Gelatin, Adipic Acid (for Tartness), Contains Less than 2% of Artificial Flavor, Disodium Phosphate and Sodium Citrate (Control Acidity), Fumaric Acid (for Tartness), Yellow 5, Blue 1, BHA (Preservative).

Here we see that Jell-O is a chaotic mix of extreme yang (gelatin) and extreme yin (sugar, artificial flavors, and synthetic dyes.)

The addiction to extreme yin, usually in the form of sugar, is easy to understand. It comes from over consumption of yang extremes like animal food and salt. However, usually these extremes are contained in separate foods or substances, for example, hamburgers and Coke, hot dogs and beer, fried chicken and mashed potatoes, and eggs and ketchup.

The fact that the Jell-O formula contains both extremes makes it especially problematic. The yang extreme—gelatin—sets up the strong craving for the opposite extreme. The sugar and artificial flavors partially satisfy the craving while the acids that produce tartness leave the person wanting more.

The craving thus reinforces and feeds upon itself. Thus, eating more satisfies the craving for Jell-O. No other food is needed. Of course, such an extreme cycle would lead to total hardening and rigidity on the one hand, and malnutrition and depletion on the other. The cool temperature and semi-solid texture are yin and further counterbalance the extreme yang of animal gelatin.

Soft drinks employ the same strategy. In addition to plenty of sugar (extreme yin) or high fructose corn syrup (even more yin), Coca Cola contains sodium, which is extremely yang. Chips are another example. They contain both extreme yin (oil) and extreme yang (salt) in an uneven balance. Salt reinforces the craving for oil and oil reinforces the craving for salt. It is difficult to stop eating chips once you've eaten the first one.

Apparently, the modern food industry has learned how to apply the law of opposites in order to drive consumption. Such an ingenious application of yin and yang would be admirable if it weren't for the fact these products have had such a devastating effect on public health. (Read the book, *Salt, Sugar, Fat* by Michael Moss for a description of food industry strategies aimed at addicting consumers to their products.)

Animal gelatin is used in a variety of products, which, like Jell-O, hide their gruesome origin behind the veneer of sweetness, frivolity, and innocence. Many of these products are marketed to children. Obvious junk foods like marshmallows, candy corn, and Peeps all contain gelatin, as do semi-legitimate foods like frozen vegetables. Why would anyone want to ruin vegetables—even frozen ones—by adding gelatin? To avoid gelatin, it is important to read the labels on processed foods or brand name products. Let's look at gummy bears, a popular candy eaten around the world. Gummy bears are made from a mixture of sugar, glucose syrup, starch, flavoring, food coloring, citric acid, and gelatin. Like Jell-O, gummy bears are a zany mix of extremes. Developed originally in Germany, gummy bears raise a number of red flags. These include concerns that their sugar content contributes to tooth decay and fears that the dyes used in coloring them are carcinogenic.

There is also concern that the prions that cause mad cow disease could be hiding in the gelatin and transferred to humans. Aside from these concerns, remember that gummy bears are made from the central core of cows and pigs. Their yang effects go deep and last for years.

Kanten, or agar, a gelatinous substance made from a red sea algae known as tengusa, offers a healthy vegan alternative to Jell-O (see next chapter.) The process of making kanten is natural and labor intensive. It makes use of natural sunlight and freezing cold to turn the thick gel of the cooked seaweed into dry strips. Only a handful of producers still produce kanten in the traditional way. Agar is used as an ingredient in many dishes. In macrobiotic cooking we use it to prepare a variety of cooling and refreshing desserts, which have the texture and feel of Jell-O without the harmful ingredients. In the next chapter, we take a closer look at the role of kanten in a plant-based macrobiotic diet.

I know of nothing else in medicine that can come
close to what a plant-based diet can do. In theory, if
everyone were to adopt this, I really believe we can
cut health care costs by seventy to eighty percent.
That's amazing. And it all comes from understanding
nutrition, applying nutrition, and just watching the
results.

T. Colin Campbell

11 KUZU AND KANTEN

Lately I've been referring to kuzu and kanten as the "crown jewels" of macrobiotics. That designation is justified for several reasons. First, both of these natural foods are made from wild crafted ingredients. They are 100% natural and organic. The method of processing them is labor-intensive and time-consuming. Kuzu is a natural root starch thickener; kanten is a naturally gelling sea vegetable flake, bar, or strip. Kanten is sometimes referred to as "agar" in English. Both are used often in macrobiotic cooking.

According to the Mitoku web site (Mitoku.com) it takes 120 days to make high quality Akizuki kuzu:

> The process begins in December, when the kuzu plant has focused its energy back down underground and its roots are swollen with starch. The backbreaking work of hand digging roots in the mountains and backpacking them to the nearest road continues until spring. The method of separating the starch from the fibrous kuzu root requires that the root be cleaned, cut, mashed, and then washed repeatedly in cold water.

The crude paste is washed and filtered through silk screens many times to remove plant fibers and bitter tannins. After settling, the kuzu paste is again dissolved in cold water and filtered. The washing, filtering, and settling process continue until a pure white, clay-like starch is formed. The starch is cut into 6-inch thick blocks and placed in paper-lined boxes to dry for about sixty days. The drying process is critical.

Kuzu cannot be dried in direct sunshine or heated ovens, as this will affect the purity of its color and impair its jelling qualities. Oven drying makes the kuzu too brittle and hard to dissolve in water. Proper drying takes place in a long wooden shed with large windows that are opened to circulate the air. Every few days, the boxes of kuzu are moved around to make sure each block dries evenly. When properly dried, each block of kuzu should contain about 16 percent moisture. Once dried, Akizuki kuzu is carefully dusted with a soft hairbrush, crumbled, and packaged.

A traditional labor-intensive process also produces kanten. Kanten is produced from a species of red sea algae known as "tengusa." Once again, according to Mitoku:

The natural snow-dried method begins on Japan's coast, where certain red sea vegetables are harvested in the fall and sun-dried. The dried sea vegetables are bundled and taken up to the Mizoguchi shop to be made into kanten during the cold winter months. Beginning in December, the sea vegetables are placed in a large cauldron with water and allowed to cook down for several hours. The resulting gel is allowed to cool. It is then cut into blocks, arranged on bamboo trays, and set outside on snow-covered rice paddies.

Moisture in the gelatin freezes each night then thaws during the day. In about ten days, all the moisture is gone and the light, flaky bars of pure kanten remain. The crisp, porous, feather-light bars are then shaved into fine flakes and packaged.

The second reason I refer to these foods as crown jewels is because of their health benefits. They are powerful regulators of our digestive health. Let us use yin and yang to understand this clearly. As we can see in the photo, kuzu is a deep root. Harvest begins in December, when yang energy is at its peak and gathers deep within the root.

Kuzu has a warming effect on the body. All in all, kuzu has strong yang properties. Kanten, on the other hand, is made from sea algae that are dispersed in the ocean. It has cooling properties. Thus kanten is a more yin product.

In terms of digestion and elimination, constipation and diarrhea are the opposite of one another. Constipation is most often caused by stagnation and blockage in the lower colon resulting from too much meat and animal food and not enough fiber. That type of constipation is strongly yang. Diarrhea or loose stools have the opposite cause. The intestines are watery and loose, or yin. Kuzu and kanten can help remedy these conditions. Because it has yang consolidating and congealing effects, kuzu is an effective remedy for diarrhea, including the severe diarrhea resulting from inflammatory bowel disease such as ulcerative colitis.

Kuzu helps stabilize overactive energy in the colon and make the bowel movement firmer. These yang effects are made more powerful by tweaking the kuzu toward yang; in other words, by imparting a salty flavor to it. This traditional remedy is known as Ume-Sho-Kuzu.

We make this remedy by combining umeboshi plum (which has a strong salty-sour taste, powerful antibacterial effects, and helps promote an alkaline condition in the body) with hot kuzu tea. The tea is seasoned lightly with organic shoyu or soy sauce, which also has a salty flavor. Because it is served hot, it helps warm the body in cold weather.

Kanten, being yin—lubricating, relaxing, and hydrating—is an effective remedy for yang constipation. It was traditionally used as a natural laxative with no adverse side effects. It is especially beneficial when combined with apple cider, which also has a mild laxative effect. By using apple cider (or other local organic fruit juice) as a base, we are tweaking the kanten to provide a yin effect. Once again, this is helpful in remedying an over-yang condition. Kanten is frequently served chilled or at room temperature. It is used in Japan to cool the body during the heat of summer. Kuzu and kanten can also be tweaked in the opposite way. For example we can tweak hot kuzu tea toward yin, and can tweak cool or room temperature kanten toward yang. The more yin kuzu preparation is known as Ame, or "sweet" kuzu.

We prepare Ame Kuzu by substituting apple cider for water in the recipe, while eliminating the umeboshi and shoyu. Or it can be prepared with water and kuzu, with brown rice syrup added for sweetness.

A tablespoonful of brown rice syrup is added to the kuzu tea once it becomes hot. Sweet kuzu is helpful in balancing and relieving the over-yang condition known as hypoglycemia, or low blood sugar. Sweet kuzu also helps relieve stress and tension. A cup of hot Ame Kuzu before bed can help a person with low blood sugar sleep peacefully through the night.

Sweet kuzu also helps alleviate the craving for sugar and other sweets, as well as the craving for alcohol. Studies in China show the successful treatment of alcohol addiction through the use of kuzu.

Just as yang kuzu can be tweaked toward yin; yin kanten can be tweaked toward yang. This is achieved by using vegetables, beans, or other non-fruit ingredients, or by serving the kanten at room temperature. In Japan azuki bean and matcha (green tea) kanten are popular treats. Macrobiotic chefs also prepare vegetable aspics using such things as cooked split peas, cooked carrot, zucchini, daikon, radish, and other vegetables in an unsweetened kanten base.

Aspic would be better than fruit kanten for someone with a yin condition such as anemia, hypothyroid, or a person who is always chilly.

Aspic is less cooling than fruit kanten and may be more appropriate than fruit kanten in cold weather. I encourage everyone to experiment with and enjoy these marvelously healthful foods. Please discover why they truly can be called the crown jewels of macrobiotics. Below is a summary of how to prepare these useful and effective dishes.

Ume Sho Kuzu

Ume Sho Kuzu is a standard drink used to strengthen digestion, restore energy, reduce inflammation, and help the body discharge acidity.

1. Dissolve one or two heaping teaspoons of kuzu in two to three teaspoons of cold water.
2. Add one cup of cold water to the dissolved kuzu.
3. Bring to a boil over a medium flame, stirring constantly to avoid lumping, until the liquid becomes translucent. Reduce the flame to low.
4. Add the pulp of one-half to one umeboshi plum.
5. Add several drops to one teaspoon of shoyu/soy sauce and stir gently. Simmer for 2-3 minutes. Drink hot.

Ame (Sweet) Kuzu

Adding brown rice syrup to the kuzu drink produces a sweet soothing beverage that helps relax tension and ease the craving for sweets, simple sugars, and alcohol. Taken before bed it helps promote deep relaxing sleep.

1. Dilute one tablespoonful of kuzu in several tablespoons cold water.
2. Place one cup of cold water in a saucepan and add the diluted kuzu, mixing thoroughly.
3. Place on a medium to high flame. Stir constantly to prevent clumping.
4. Add one tablespoon brown rice syrup to the hot liquid and stir in.
5. When the kuzu becomes thick and clear, pour into a cup or bowl and drink hot.

You may substitute organic apple juice or cider for water in the recipe. Omit the brown rice syrup.

Apple Kanten

Kanten is a refreshing jelled dish that cools and relaxes the body and promotes regular elimination. It has natural laxative properties.

1. Place organic apple juice or cider in a saucepan and add kanten flakes. Stir to distribute evenly.
2. Bring to a boil and simmer until the flakes are thoroughly dissolved.
3 Continue to simmer on a low to medium flame for about ten minutes, gently stirring throughout.
4. Pour into individual cups or shallow bowls, ideally with two to three inches of hot kanten liquid.

5. Set aside or place in refrigerator until completely jelled (about ½-hour in refrigerator.) Serve as is. Kanten can be enjoyed as a snack between meals or at the end of a meal as dessert.

Fresh seasonal fruit, such as melon, berries, apple, pear, etc. may be added to kanten. Slice the fruit as needed and place at the bottom of a cup or bowl. Pour hot kanten liquid over the fruit and jell as suggested above.

12 THE RICE CYCLE

In the first chapter, we saw how the cycle of nutritional energy corresponds to the five transformations, or stages of change. This pattern is repeated throughout the natural world. The natural world is governed by cycles, and these cycles are animated by yin and yang and the five transformations. Let us now see how the growth cycle of rice reflects this pattern.

In the spring, yin or upward energy is dominant. Rice seeds are germinated indoors in small beds. The seeds put out roots while sprouts emerge and begin to shoot upward. Green, the color of the rice seedlings, is the color of spring. As the shoots grow, the rice paddy, which was dry over the winter, is flooded. When the shoots reach a height above the water level, they are taken outside and transplanted in evenly spaced rows. Transplantation was traditionally done by hand and considered one of the most important events of the year. The rows in the paddy provide space for the plants to grow and produce the maximum amount of seeds.

Interestingly, like other cereals, rice will grow on dry land. The reason for the water-filled paddy is twofold. First, flooding eliminates weeds that could serve as competition for the rice. Second, the water absorbs heat during the day. It retains heat during cool spring nights. Like a blanket, it keeps the seedlings warm, allowing them to survive cool nighttime temperatures. What an ingenious system! This method of growing rice is truly sustainable. It has essentially continued unchanged for thousands of years. Ancient people gave the upward energy of spring the iconic name, "Tree." The tree icon conjures an image of things growing up above the ground. The germinating and planting stages are perfect examples of this tree energy.

Through the spring and into summer, the rice continues growing. Tadpoles appear in the paddy, while tiny green frogs appear on the rice plants. Their song enlivens the rice field. Under the influence of expansive force, the rice plant matures and reaches a height of 3 to 4 feet. It produces a reproductive stem known as a *tiller*. As expansive force reaches a peak, the stem will produce a flower head, often referred to as a *spike*. Each spike will then produce up to 150 tiny flowers. Once pollinated, the flowers form seeds. Ancient people gave the highly expansive energy of summer the iconic name "Fire." The fire icon generates an image of things reaching their peak of expansion.

Flowers represent the peak of expansive energy. At this time, dragonflies appear and dart in and out of the rice paddy. Their distinctive buzz becomes part of the natural ecosystem.

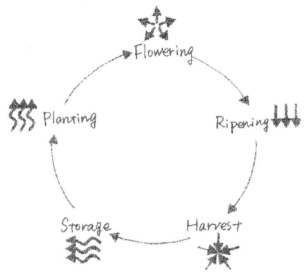

Illustration by by Naomi Ichikawa Esko

Once pollinated, each flower produces seeds. Seed formation is the beginning of the process in which the yin expansive energy of summer begins to move in the opposite, or downward direction. In comparison to flowers, seeds are highly compact or yang. Next comes the ripening stage in which the seeds turn golden brown. This occurs in late summer amidst an overall trend toward yang downward energy.

Ancient people gave the energy of late summer the iconic name "Soil." The soil icon conjures the image of soil or earth, which are dense and compact in relation to tree or fire. As we enter autumn, the seeds become highly compact. Energy is being stored in each grain.

The heads bend down due to increasingly contractive energy in the environment. Finally at the peak of ripening, the rice is ready for harvest.

At that time, the rice paddy is drained. The rice is hand cut with curved metal knives, stacked, bundled, and hung upside down to dry. Rice harvest is a very important time of year, equal to rice planting in traditional societies. Following harvest, people held festivals to celebrate the new crop and enjoy the abundance of nature.

Ancient people gave the highly condensed energy of autumn the iconic name "Metal." Metal is the most yang or condensed stage in the cycle of the seasons. The seasonal cycle is known as the "five transformations." At harvest, the rice undergoes a complete reversal in polarity. The grains, which point upward during the growing process, are now cut and hung upside down, facing the earth. Once the rice has dried, it is then threshed, or separated from the stalk. The threshed grains are then collected and stored in sacks. The rice initially has its outer coat, or husk, attached. Some of this rice is put aside as seed for the next season. Some is hulled, meaning the inedible coat is removed.

Freshly hulled brown rice has the strongest life energy of any variety of rice. The stage in which rice is stored, either for seed or in the pantry as food, corresponds to the dormant season of winter. Ancient people gave that season the iconic name "Water." Water represents a phase in which atmospheric energy floats between heaven and earth, or yang and yin.

Winter is the time of rest and dormancy in preparation for the rising and awakening energy of the coming spring. In the spring, the cycle begins again.

The Rice Cycle is a reflection of universal order. We can understand this more clearly when we examine the Oriental concept of "Ki." Ki is defined as life energy. Some consider it to be the primal force that animates the universe. It is the invisible electric and magnetic force that powers galaxies, stars, planets, elements, atoms, and biological life, including plants and animals. The pathways of Ki in the human body were mapped long ago. These pathways are the chakras studied in yoga philosophy and the meridians used in Chinese medicine.

"Chakra" is an ancient Sanskrit word for "wheel." The chakras are found along a central energy core running deep within the body. This invisible energy line connects heaven and earth. Seven energy centers, or chakras, appear along this line.

The energy core and chakras are the primary source of the life energy that animates our biological, emotional, mental, and even spiritual functions. The chakras disperse life energy from the central core out toward the surface. Ki runs along invisible lines or channels just below the skin. These are the meridians used in acupuncture, Shiatsu, and other forms of Oriental medicine. Ki also animates plants. Seeds are especially concentrated forms of energy. One thousand year-old grains have been known to sprout and grow, in an example of incredibly powerful life force.

The character for "Ki."
Calligraphy by Naomi Ichikawa Esko

The Chinese character, or Kanji, for "Ki" is made up of two parts. The horizontal lines in the upper portion envelop and cover the lines at the lower left. The upper lines denote the invisible energy or movement of the universe; the ultimate source of all creation or manifestation.

This invisible motion takes the form of never-ending expansion. The vertical and horizontal lines in the lower section represent the appearance of two complementary-opposite forces, or yin and yang.

The vertical and horizontal lines form a cross. From the two poles (yin and yang), four cardinal points are produced. Then a mid-point arises between each of the four sets of cardinal points, producing eight divisions. The appearance of the first two lines, or yin and yang, sets in motion universal and eternal cycles of change.

These cycles produce ceaseless motion between the two poles of expansion (yin) and contraction (yang), including cycles of growth and decay, rising and falling, movement and rest. Throughout the universe, this ceaseless alternation assumes the pattern of a rotating spiral. From our vantage point on earth, we experience yin and yang as the intersection of time and space. The four cardinal directions, North and South, East and West, correspond to the four cardinal points, as do the four seasons winter and summer, spring and fall.

We constantly move back and forth between the cardinal directions, while cycling constantly between day and night, summer and winter, morning and afternoon, and spring and fall. Interestingly enough, the lines at the lower left are translated as "rice." Rice and other cereals contain strong Ki or life energy.

They are the product of the seasonal cycle through which the energies of yin and yang manifest. Their awns, or hair-like growths that project from each grain, are delicate antennae pointing toward the cosmos. These tiny antennae conduct energy and information from the cosmos itself. Eating them strengthens not only our life energy, but helps reveal our universal mind.

13 FOOD IS INFORMATION

All food is information. When you put food in your mouth, the mouth functions as an information-detecting unit. Normally, when people process information from food, what is the main thing being received, what is the main information? Taste. The information is highly sensorial. Because they are taking food with such hyper enhanced taste, sensory pleasure is the limit of their information. Most people like ice cream. Because the information they get from ice cream is overwhelmingly pleasurable. And of course people become addicted to that.

At MacDonald's they perform all kinds of tricks to make their food satisfying and addictive. They have entire divisions of people working to make the food have a certain taste, texture, or feel in the mouth. The majority of people today are overwhelmed by sensory information when they eat. How about macrobiotic people? You start to take information beyond the sensory level. All kinds of new information start to come in.

When you eat brown rice, what kind of information are you getting, besides wonderful taste and wonderful chew-ability? If you visit the rice field at South River Miso or see whole grains growing in the field, you see they have tiny hairs coming up from each grain. These tiny hairs are called "awns." They are beautifully delicate hairs.

When the grains are growing they function as tiny antenna pointing to the cosmos. The antennae conduct signals, energy, and information from the cosmos. When you eat brown rice and other whole grains you are receiving cosmic force from the whole universe. Naturally that conditions your thinking, your view. Your view becomes very whole. You see the whole universe. You are able to see the whole picture. Your thinking is not fragmented or partial but holistic and universal. What happens when you eat a food such as turkey? I have eaten poultry only half-dozen or so times in the past forty years.

Several years ago I went to my son and daughter-in-law's house for Thanksgiving. My daughter-in-law's parents came to dinner. They are very nice people. They brought a turkey, probably because they felt sorry for their grandchildren who were being served a turkey-free, plant-based meal. To be polite and sociable and to join in, I decided to try a small piece. I tried to take the smallest piece possible; meanwhile my in-laws were watching and smiling.

Like all grains, barley projects antenna-like awns.

As soon as the turkey entered my mouth, information came flooding in. Once again the mouth is our information receiver or information-decoding unit. The information I received was one level above the sensory level. The first bit of data, received in nanoseconds, processed beyond the speed of the highest speed computer, was on the emotional level, above that of sensory input. It was an unbelievable feeling of sadness and misery. Why misery?

The sensation of misery arose because that creature endured a very miserable life and suffered a very miserable death. (You can confirm that by viewing YouTube videos documenting the conditions in factory farms.)

Modern livestock are so sick that high doses of antibiotics are required to keep them alive. They are fed hormones to speed growth and are confined in small dark spaces; never seeing the sun. How does a sick and miserable factory-farmed turkey compare to a turkey that roams freely in the wild? The wild turkey is free, vital, and healthy. Even if hunted, the wild turkey is free up until the moment of death, unlike the confined, sick, factory-farmed turkey.

The second bit of information took the form of a slight taste of antiseptic chemicals such as those used in a hospital or operating room. That sense arose because of the antibiotics being feed to the turkeys as well as the highly toxic chemicals used to disinfect the pathological environment of the slaughterhouse.

The third bit of information was the feeling that, when eaten on a regular basis, the hard tough protein and fatty gristle comprising the turkey would lead to the formation of a cyst or tumor. These unnatural growths are formed by protein and fat. Needless to say, I learned much from that small piece of turkey.

Unlike the positive information received from brown rice and other whole grains, the information I received from the turkey was negative.

What kind of information are people channeling today? People are receiving very unhappy, unhealthy, and often violent information. Modern livestock suffer a violent death. (The word "carnivore" shares the same root as the word "carnage.")

This information is low grade compared to the information received from whole grains and vegetables. What do we see in our world? We see constant war and violence, with seemingly no end in sight.

The Japanese character for "peace" or "Wa." The symbol at left denotes "cereal grain," that at right denotes "mouth."
Calligraphy by Naomi Ichikawa Esko

When we eat grains we channel information from the cosmos. What type of society does grain-eating produce? Far Eastern people gave us a clue with their character for the word "peace."

The character for peace is pronounced "Wa." It is a combination of characters that represent "cereal grain" and "mouth." Ancient people were telling us that not only do we as individuals gain physical, mental, and spiritual health when we eat grain as our main food, but that when grain becomes the principal food of society, our entire culture becomes peaceful.

Eating grain equals channeling energy and information from the cosmos. At present, our North Pole is approaching the spiritual energy of the Milky Way. As a result, we have an unprecedented opportunity to create a sustainable spiritual civilization with values that are the opposite of the values that prevail today. The important thing is for everyone to eat grain as main food and begin channeling the energy and information coming from the galaxy and from the universe as a whole. That enables us to see beyond our immediate world, which is governed by the unhappy and unhealthy energy coming from animal foods. We see beyond the present and can imagine a peaceful and prosperous future for all humanity.

People who eat grains as their main food and who establish health and a peaceful mind are able to guide this transition. Because they are channeling energy from the cosmos, they see the whole view, perceive the peaceful universe as it is, and are able to guide humanity toward the realization of that peaceful reality on planet earth.

14 SAVING THE RAINFOREST

Nowhere are the repercussions of the modern diet more apparent than in the wholesale destruction of tropical rainforests. The problem was brought to international attention this summer with the massive wildfires in the Amazon and elsewhere. Many previously unaware people gained an awareness of the role of the modern diet—especially the consumption of beef—on rainforest destruction.

The native peoples of South America refer to the rainforest as the "lungs of the earth." Oxygen is a more yin or expansive gas, carbon dioxide is more yang or contractive. Expansive force caused by earth's rotation and constant sunshine is strong at the equator. These powerful energies cause vegetation and animal life to become lush and expanded. Species proliferate, leading to an amazing range of biodiversity. Besides being a repository for an incredible array of species, tropical rainforests are like huge processing plants that release oxygen into the atmosphere.

The rainforests also absorb a tremendous amount of carbon dioxide. Sadly, modern civilization has launched all-out war on this precious natural resource. An area of the earth's rainforests disappears every second. Cattle ranching is the leading cause of this destruction. Many years ago, Al Gore talked about this tragedy in his seminal book, *Earth in the Balance*:

> As it happens, some of the most disturbing images of environmental destruction can be found exactly halfway between the North and South Poles—precisely at the equator in Brazil—where billowing clouds of smoke regularly blacken the sky above the immense but now threatened Amazon rainforest. Acre by acre, the rainforest is being burned to create fast pasture for fast-food beef, with more than one Tennessee's-worth of rainforest being slashed and burned each year.

The tropical ecology is delicate and fragile. Ninety-five percent of the soil's nutrients exist above the ground as plant life. (That ratio is reversed in the temperate zones, where 95% of the available nutrients are found in the soil, and 5% in the forest itself.) Before modern civilization there were about 6 million square miles of tropical rainforest on the planet. That amount has now been reduced by half, to about 3 million square miles. At current rates of destruction, all of the tropical rainforests will vanish by mid-century. Humanity will no longer inhabit a lush blue-green planet. The consequences of this manmade catastrophe are incalculable.

Changing to a plant-based diet is perhaps the single most important step that individuals can take to halt destruction of the rainforest. A plant-based macrobiotic diet offers a sustainable alternative to this destructive trend. Macrobiotic nutrition is thus an essential element in achieving both personal and planetary health. It may be the key to preserving our planetary home.

The Gods created certain kinds of beings to replenish our bodies; they are the trees and the plants and the seeds.

Plato

ABOUT THE AUTHOR

Edward Esko is one of the world's leading teachers and authors on macrobiotics. He is married to Naomi Ichikawa Esko, also a teacher of macrobiotics. Edward worked for many years as an associate of Michio Kushi and served as senior faculty and director of education for the East West Foundation and the Kushi Institute.

He is the founder of the International Macrobiotic Institute, the Kushi School of New York, and Berkshire Holistic Associates. In addition to numerous articles and essays for a variety of periodicals, he is the author of over a dozen books, including *Chakras & Meridians* (with Michio Kushi.) He lives in Western Massachusetts where he conducts the popular Macrobiotic Online Course. You can contact him at: edwardesko@gmail.com.

Made in the USA
Middletown, DE
19 November 2019

79022180R00051